The Concise Guide to
Cupcakes

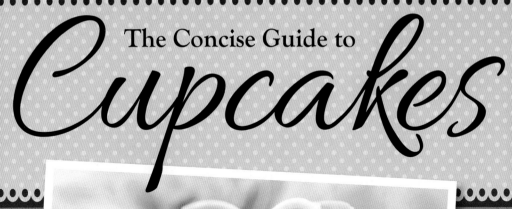

igloobooks

Published in 2014
by Igloo Books Ltd
Cottage Farm
Sywell
NN6 0BJ
www.igloobooks.com

HUN001 0314
2 4 6 8 10 9 7 5 3 1
ISBN 978-1-78197-962-4

Recipe development and photography by PhotoCuisine and CakeyPigg

Printed and manufactured in China

The Concise Guide to
Cupcakes

Contents

Tools and Equipment

Whilst some cupcakes are very simple to decorate and require very little specialist equipment, there are others that will require you to have some more specialist tools to hand.

Icing Cutters

Cutters come in many different shapes and sizes, from simple circular cutters through to novelty shapes and push out cutters that also pattern the icing. Cutters enable you to make much more precise shapes for decorating your cupcakes, and it's worth investing in a range of different sizes and shapes and building a collection up over time.

Piping Bags and Nozzles

A sugarcraft and cupcake decorating staple, the cake decorator should have a good selection of piping bags and nozzles of various sizes to enable them to pipe different effects and different icings onto cupcakes.

Foam Modelling Mats

These enable the cake decorator to easily and hygienically work with sugarpaste. The mat acts as a soft base to model delicate elements of sugarcraft, and also acts as a useful place to allow sugarcraft shapes to harden.

Cake Polishers and Rolling Pi

In order to get a professional finish to your icing work, you'll need cake polishers to smooth out uneven blemishes in your fondant icing, and also to prepare flat even surfaces in your fondant icing. Rolling pins of different sizes and with thickness guides fitted will enable you to work with larger and smaller pieces of fondant, to create uniform thicknesses.

Pump Action Sugarpaste Gun

Used to create a variety of fondant effects, where the consistency of the icing is too thick for standard piping. The guns come with a variety of apertures to create different shaped fondant ropes, hair, scallops and a huge range of fondant effects.

Sugarcraft Tools

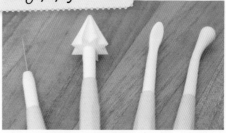

Bone tool: ideal for thinning and smoothing the edges of leaves, flower petals and frills.

Ball tool: a great tool to cup and shape leaves, petals and frills. The small end is ideal for creating detail on marzipan figures.

Serrated and tapered cone tool: used to indent into paste to create a cone shaped hollow, ideal for modelling marzipan or fondant fruits such as apples. The serrated cone is good for creating detailed and realistic throats of flowers.

Scriber tool: is used for transcribing designs onto sugar or fondant plaques, royal icing, sugarpaste or chocolate. The scriber tool is most useful to mark outlines of designs that you intend to pipe or paint onto a cake.

Paint Brushes

A clean set of paintbrushes are an essential tool for the cupcake decorator, and can be used for painting directly onto icing, sticking decorations to cupcakes, and manipulating and texturing sugarpaste. Always wash and dry your brushes thoroughly after use to prevent them from clogging.

Food Colouring

There are many different types and colours of food colourings using both natural and artificial ingredients. Liquid, gel and dry powder colourings are available and enable the cupcake decorator to colour soft and hard fondants, cakes and sugar.

Basic Recipes and Techniques

Vanilla Cupcakes

Makes: **10-12**
Preparation: **15 minutes**
Cooking time: **22 minutes**

Ingredients

125 g / 4 ½ oz / ½ cup butter, unsalted, softened
125 g / 4 ½ oz / ½ cup caster (superfine) sugar
2 eggs
½ tsp vanilla extract
125 g / 4 ½ oz / 1 cup self-raising flour
3 tbsp milk

1

- Preheat the oven to 180°C (160° fan) / 350F / gas 4 and line a cupcake tin with paper cases.

2

- Beat butter and sugar together until light and fluffy.
- Whisk in vanilla and eggs one by one.

3

- Gently mix in flour, adding milk.
- Spoon cupcake mix into each paper case.

4

- Bake for 18-22 minutes. Test with a wooden toothpick, if it comes out clean, the cake is done.
- Place on wire rack to cool.

Chocolate Cupcakes

Makes: **10-12**
Preparation: **15 minutes**
Cooking time: **22 minutes**

Ingredients

125 g / 4 ½ oz / ½ cup butter, unsalted, softened
125 g / 4 ½ oz / ½ cup caster (superfine) sugar
2 eggs
½ tsp vanilla extract
125 g / 4 ½ oz / 1 cup self-raising flour
2 tbsp cocoa powder
3 tbsp milk

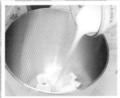

1

- Preheat the oven to 180°C (160° fan) / 350F / gas 4 and line a cupcake tin with paper cases.

2

- Beat butter and sugar together until light and fluffy.
- Whisk in vanilla and eggs one by one.

3

- Gently mix in flour and cocoa powder, adding milk.
- Spoon cupcake mix into each paper case.

4

- Bake for 18-22 minutes. Test with a wooden toothpick, if it comes out clean, the cake is done.
- Place on wire rack to cool.

Chocolate Chip Cupcakes

Makes: **10-12**
Preparation: **15 minutes**
Cooking time: **22 minutes**

Ingredients

125 g / 4 ½ oz / ½ cup butter, unsalted, softened
125 g / 4 ½ oz / ½ cup caster (superfine) sugar
2 eggs
½ tsp vanilla extract
125 g / 4 ½ oz / 1 cup self-raising flour
3 tbsp milk
125 g / 4 ½ oz / 1 cup chocolate chips

1

- Preheat the oven to 180°C (160° fan) / 350F / gas 4 and line a cupcake tin with paper cases.

2

- Beat butter and sugar together until light and fluffy.
- Whisk in vanilla and eggs one by one.

3

- Gently mix in flour, adding milk.
- Mix in the chocolate chips.
- Spoon cupcake mix into each paper case.

4

- Bake for 18-22 minutes. Test with a wooden toothpick, if it comes out clean, the cake is done.
- Place on wire rack to cool.

Lemon Cupcakes

Makes: **10-12**
Preparation: **15 minutes**
Cooking time: **22 minutes**

Ingredients

125 g / 4 ½ oz / ½ cup butter, unsalted, softened
125 g / 4 ½ oz / ½ cup caster (superfine) sugar
2 eggs
½ tsp vanilla extract / lemon, juiced
125 g / 4 ½ oz / 1 cup self-raising flour
3 tbsp milk

1

- Preheat the oven to 180°C (160° fan) / 350F / gas 4 and line a cupcake tin with paper cases.

2

- Beat butter and sugar together until light and fluffy.
- Whisk in vanilla and eggs one by one.

3

- Gently mix in flour, adding milk.
- Stir in the lemon juice.
- Spoon cupcake mix into each paper case.

4

- Bake for 18-22 minutes. Test with a wooden toothpick, if it comes out clean, the cake is done.
- Place on wire rack to cool.

Plain Buttercream

Makes: **enough to ice 12 cupcakes**
Preparation: **5 minutes**

Ingredients

100 g / 3 ½ oz / ½ cup butter, at room temperature
200 g / 7 oz / 2 cups icing (confectioners') sugar, sieved

1

- Cut the butter into small cubes with a sharp knife and transfer it to a mixing bowl.

2

- Beat the butter vigorously until smooth with a spoon or electric whisk.

3

- Weigh the icing sugar into the bowl.

4

- Beat in the icing sugar with a wooden spoon or electric whisk until the mixture is pale and smoothly combined.

Lemon Buttercream

Beat the zest and juice of half a lemon into the buttercream icing after incorporating the icing sugar. You can also colour the icing with a few drops of pale yellow food colouring.

Royal Icing

Makes: **enough to ice 12 cupcakes**
Preparation: **10 minutes**

Ingredients

200 g / 7 oz / 2 cups icing (confectioners') sugar
1 egg white

1

- Weigh out the icing sugar, then sieve it to remove any lumps.

2

- Separate the egg and transfer the egg white to a clean, grease-free mixing bowl.

3

- Whisk the egg white until foamy, then gradually incorporate the icing sugar.
- Whisk the icing for 3 – 4 minutes or until smooth and thick.

Royal Icing with Glycerine

To make royal icing that stays soft for longer, whisk ½ tsp of glycerine into the icing after incorporating the sugar.

Piping Work

Piping icing can be a daunting task for anyone new to decorating cupcakes. It's a skill that takes a bit of practice to get right but once mastered will allow the cupcake decorator to perform a wide range of creative tasks including scalloping, swags, ropes, flowers, leaves and many other effects.

How to practise piping royal icing

Make the royal icing as per the recipe in the previous pages, and ensure that its kept in an airtight container to prevent it from hardening and drying out. The royal icing needs to be stiff enough to hold its form yet malleable enough to be piped through a small piping nozzle.

1

- You can make a piping bag by rolling greaseproof paper into a cone, snipping off the pointed end and inserting a piping nozzle.

2

3

- Secure with a piping bag collar. Fill your piping bag with buttercream, royal icing, or your desired topping.

- Practise swirls, swags and dotting on some greaseproof paper. You can experiment in creating different effects with different nozzles, until you feel confident enough to pipe the patterns onto your cupcakes.

Fondant Icing Work

Fondant icing underpins many different cake decorating techniques, and is a durable, malleable and extremely versatile material. It can be used to ice cupcakes, make novelty figures, flowers plaques and decorations.

Fondant can be purchased at most supermarkets and all good cake decorating shops. Like marzipan its worth buying good quality fondant as it will keep for longer.

Fondant icing can be easily coloured using food colourings, and will harden when left open to the air to make a smooth surface ideal for decorating and painting.

Fondant icing is available in many different colours and if you want to save time, buy ready coloured fondant in the shades you need.

Remember to tightly wrap the fondant in clingfilm once opened to prevent it hardening.

How to use fondant icing

1

2

- Knead the block of fondant on a silicon mat or surface dusted with icing sugar until its soft and malleable, this will make it easier to roll and use for modelling.

- If you're colouring your fondant, use gel food colouring to colour the icing. Add a little at a time and knead it into the fondant until you reach the desired colour. Knead the colour into the fondant until the icing is a uniform colour.

- To cover a cupcake, measure the diameter / width and ensure that you have enough fondant rolled out to cover the tops of the cupcakes. Use a cookie cutter to cut out perfect circles.

- When rolled and cut out, use a palette knife or plastic scraper to drape the fondant evenly over the cupcakes.

3

4

- Smooth over the cupcake using your hands.
- You can gently use cake buffers dusted with a little icing sugar to obtain a smooth professional finish.

- Rolled fondant can be used to make cut out shapes and plaques.

Children's

Butterfly Cupcakes

Makes: **12**
Preparation time: **1 hour 10 minutes**
Cooking time: **15 - 20 minutes**
Setting time: **overnight**

Ingredients

12 chocolate cupcakes

To decorate

110 g / 4 oz ready to roll fondant icing

orange food colouring powder

100 g / 3 ½ oz / ½ cup butter, softened

200 g / 7 oz / 2 cups icing
(confectioners') sugar

½ tsp vanilla extract

1

- Take 12 chocolate cupcakes and arrange them on a work surface ready to decorate.
- Roll out the fondant icing and cut out 12 butterfly shapes.

2

- Fold a piece of card in half to make a 'v' shape and lay the butterflies down the centre. Leave to set and harden overnight.

3

- Put a little orange food colouring powder in a plastic tray and add a few drops of water to make a paint.

4

- Paint the edge of the wings and the body onto the butterflies then add a spot to each wing.
- Beat the butter until smooth, then gradually whisk in the icing sugar, vanilla extract and a little of the orange food colouring powder.

5

- Spoon the mixture into a piping bag, fitted with a large star nozzle. Starting in the centre, pipe the icing on in a spiral, keeping the piping bag completely vertical to produce a rose effect.

6

- Press a butterfly onto the side of each one.

Dragonfly Cupcakes
Cut out 12 dragonfly shapes and use blue and green pearlescent dusts to make the paint.

1

- Take 12 chocolate cupcakes ready to decorate.
- Beat the butter until smooth, then gradually whisk in the icing sugar and vanilla extract.
- Colour the buttercream pale green and spread half of it over the surface of the cakes.
- Spoon the rest of the buttercream into a piping bag, fitted with a plain nozzle and pipe a ring of teardrops round the edge of each cake.

2

- Colour 1 third of the fondant icing pale pink. Shape it into 12 quail's egg shapes and 48 pea-sized balls.
- Flatten 24 of the pea-sized balls and pinch one end together to make the ears.

3

- Use a little of the white fondant icing to make circles for the eyes and attach to the heads. Make the pupils from small circles of fondant icing, coloured with blue food colouring and attach with water.

4

- Use a scalpel to score in the mouth details.
- Make 2 small indentations in each head and insert the ears, securing with a little water.

5

- Shape the white icing into 12 bodies and attach a head and 2 front feet to each one with a little water.

6

- Cut the mini marshmallows in half with scissors, dipping them in icing sugar if they get too sticky.

7

- Use the sticky cut side of the marshmallows to attach them to the bodies of the sheep, then transfer each sheep to the top of a cake.

Poodle Cupcakes
Use this technique to make a poodle for the top of each cake, adding a red icing dog collar to each one.

Sheep Cupcakes

Makes: **12**
Preparation time:
1 hour 30 minutes
Cooking time:
15 - 20 minutes

Ingredients

12 chocolate cupcakes

To decorate

100 g / 3 ½ oz / ½ cup butter, softened

200 g / 7 oz / 2 cups icing (confectioners') sugar

½ tsp vanilla extract

green food colouring

300 g / 10 ½ oz ready to roll fondant icing

pink and blue food colouring

150 g / 5 ½ oz mini marshmallows

Crown Cupcakes

Makes: **12**
Preparation time: **1 hour 10 minutes**
Cooking time: **15 - 20 minutes**

Ingredients

12 lemon cupcakes

To decorate

100 g / 3 ½ oz / ½ cup butter, softened

200 g / 7 oz / 2 cups icing (confectioners') sugar

½ lemon, juiced and zest finely grated

yellow food colouring

400 g / 7 oz ready to roll fondant icing

edible silver balls

1

- Take 12 lemon cupcakes ready to decorate.
- Beat the butter until smooth, then gradually whisk in the icing sugar, lemon juice and zest and a few drops of yellow food colouring.
- Spoon the mixture into a piping bag, fitted with a large plain nozzle and pipe a swirl of buttercream on top of each cake.

2

- Colour the fondant icing yellow and roll it out on a work surface that has been lightly dusted with icing sugar.
- Cut it into 12 ribbons 2.5 cm wide, then cut a zigzag into one edge with a sharp knife.

3

- Make a dent below the centre of each point with a small ball tool.

4

- Paint a little edible flower glue into each indentation.

5

- Press a silver ball into each indentation and wait for a few minutes for the glue to work.

6

- Fold each strip round to form a crown and press them lightly into the top of the buttercream to hold the shape.

Tiara Cupcakes
Colour the fondant icing silver and cut it into tiara shapes. Decorate with multi-coloured ball jewels.

1

- Take 12 vanilla cupcakes ready to decorate.
- Use a third of the royal icing to attach a cookie to the top of each cake.

2

- Use some of the fondant icing to make 12 pairs of eyes and attach them to the cookies with a dab of royal icing.
- Colour a small piece of fondant icing purple and use it to make the pupils of the eyes, attaching them with a little water.

3

- Colour the remaining fondant icing red and roll it out on the work surface. Use a pizza wheel to cut out 12 mouth shapes and attach them to the cookies with a dab of royal icing.

4

- Use the red icing off-cuts to make the tongues and attach with a dab of water.

5

- Colour the remaining royal icing red and spoon it into a piping bag fitted with a grass piping nozzle.
- Pipe a mane of hair around each cookie, squeezing the icing onto the side of the cookie and pulling the bag away in short bursts.

Lion Cupcakes
Use the same method to pipe a brown mane onto lion faces that have been modelled out of yellow fondant icing.

Cookie Monster Cupcakes

Makes: **12**
Preparation time: **1 hour 15 minutes**
Cooking time: **15 - 20 minutes**

Ingredients

12 vanilla cupcakes

To decorate

250 g / 9 oz ready to pipe royal icing

12 cookies

100 g / 3 ½ oz ready to roll fondant icing

red and purple food colouring

Owl Cupcakes

Makes: **12**
Preparation time:
1 hour 30 minutes
Cooking time: **15 - 20 minutes**

Ingredients

12 lemon cupcakes

To decorate
400 g / 14 oz ready to roll fondant icing
blue, brown, red, purple and yellow
food colouring
icing (confectioners') sugar for dusting

1

- Take 12 lemon cupcakes ready to decorate.
- Colour half of the fondant icing pale blue. Dust the work surface lightly with icing sugar and roll out the blue icing.

2

- Use a cookie cutter the same diameter as the top of the cakes to cut out 12 circles then attach them to the top of the cakes with a dab of water.

3

- Divide the rest of the icing into 3 pieces. Colour one piece brown and one piece red. Divide the remaining piece in half and colour one piece yellow and the other purple.
- Roll out the brown icing and cut it into 12 branch shapes with a pizza wheel.

4

- Attach the branches to the cakes with a dab of water.
- Roll out the red icing and cut out 12 circles 5 cm in diameter.
- Cut the top off each circle to make a flat edge and attach them to the cakes with the flat edge at the top.

5

- Cut 24 small triangles out of the red trimmings to make the ears and attach them to the cakes.
- Roll out the yellow icing and use a small round plunger cutter to cut out 12 pairs of eyes. Attach them to the cake with a little water.
- Use the purple icing to make smaller circles for the pupils of the eyes.

6

- Knead the yellow off-cuts with the red off-cuts to make orange icing for the beaks and cut out and attach 12 small triangles.
- Use a daisy cutter to cut out 12 flowers from the purple icing, then cut them in half and use for the feet.
- Use the edge of a star cutter to emboss the feather detail on the owls' bodies.

Canary Cupcakes

Use yellow icing instead of red icing and omit the ears to make canary cupcakes.

1

- Take 12 lemon cupcakes ready to decorate.
- Beat the butter until smooth, then gradually whisk in the icing sugar, lemon juice and zest and a few drops of yellow food colouring.
- Spoon the mixture into a piping bag, fitted with a large star nozzle and pipe a swirl of buttercream on top of each cake.

2

- Colour the fondant icing brown and roll it out on a work surface that has been lightly dusted with icing sugar.

3

- Use a small gingerbread man cutter to cut out 12 gingerbread men.

4

- Use the end of a round piping nozzle to make the imprint of buttons down their chests.

5

- Use a small paint brush to paint on their shoes with some brown food colouring.

6

- Add the facial features with a plain piping nozzle, pressing it in at an angle to make a semi-circle for the mouth.
- Paint on some gloves using a small paint brush and some red food colouring.

7

- Transfer each gingerbread man to the top of a cake.

Gingerbread Lady Cupcakes

Use a gingerbread lady cutter and paint on the skirts with purple food colouring.

Gingerbread Man Cupcakes

Makes: **12**
Preparation time: **1 hour 10 minutes**
Cooking time: **15 - 20 minutes**

Ingredients

12 lemon cupcakes

To decorate

100 g / 3 ½ oz / ½ cup butter, softened

200 g / 7 oz / 2 cups icing (confectioners') sugar

½ lemon, juiced and zest finely grated

yellow, brown and red food colouring

110 g / 4 oz ready to roll fondant icing

Hedgehog Cupcakes

Makes: **12**

Preparation time:
1 hour 30 minutes

Cooking time: **15 - 20 minutes**

Ingredients

12 chocolate cupcakes

To decorate

100 g / 3 ½ oz / ½ cup butter, softened

200 g / 7 oz / 2 cups icing
(confectioners') sugar

½ tsp vanilla extract

brown and green food colouring

150 g / 5 ½ oz ready to roll fondant icing

1

- Take 12 chocolate cupcakes ready to decorate.
- Beat the butter until smooth, then gradually whisk in the icing sugar, vanilla extract and a few drops of brown food colouring.
- Spread half of the buttercream over the surface of the cakes, smoothing the surface with a palette knife.
- Spoon the rest of the buttercream into a piping bag, fitted with a large star nozzle and pipe an undulating ring on top of each cake.
- Reserve a small piece of fondant icing for the leaves and whites of the eyes and colour a third of the rest pale brown.
- Colour the rest dark brown and shape it into 12 balls.

2

- Use a clean pair of nail scissors to snip the surface of the balls into spikes.
- Use some of the pale brown fondant icing to make 36 tiny balls and set aside.

3

- Shape the rest into 12 cones and attach each one to a spikey ball with a dab of water.
- Use a third of the reserved white icing to shape 24 flat discs for the eyes and attach 2 to each hedgehog with a little water.

4

- Use 24 of the pale brown balls for the eyes, attaching with water as before.

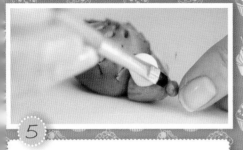

5

- Use the remaining 12 pale brown balls to make the noses.
- Colour the remaining white icing green and roll it out thinly.

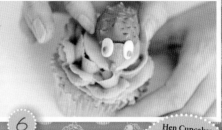

6

- Use a leaf-shaped cutter to cut out 12 leaves and lay one on the top of each cake.
- Attach the hedgehogs to the leaves with a little water.

Hen Cupcakes
Shape and snip the dark brown icing as before. Shape 12 balls to make the hens' heads and model beaks and combs out of yellow and red fondant icing.

1

- Take 12 vanilla cupcakes ready to decorate.
- Beat the butter until smooth, then gradually whisk in the icing sugar and vanilla extract. Spread the buttercream on top of the cakes, levelling the top with a palette knife.

2

- Dust the work surface lightly with icing sugar and roll out two thirds of the fondant icing.

3

- Use a cookie cutter the same diameter as the top of the cakes to cut out 12 circles.
- Attach an icing circle to the top of each cake.

4

- Colour the remaining icing black and roll it out into a large rectangle.
- Cut out 36 circles with a 3 cm diameter cutter.

5

- Use a pizza wheel to cut the circles into pentagons and reserve the trimmings.

6

- Cut the trimmings into thin strips and use them to emphasise the white hexagons in between.

Cricket Ball Cupcakes

Colour the fondant icing red and pipe the stitching on with white royal icing.

Football Cupcakes

Makes: **12**
Preparation time: **1 hour**
Cooking time:
15 - 20 minutes

Ingredients

12 vanilla cupcakes

To decorate

100 g / 3 ½ oz / ½ cup butter, softened

200 g / 7 oz / 2 cups icing (confectioners') sugar

½ tsp vanilla extract

200 g / 7 oz ready to roll fondant icing

black food colouring

Ladybird Cupcakes

Makes: **12**

Preparation time: **1 hour 15 minutes**

Cooking time: **15 - 20 minutes**

Ingredients

12 vanilla cupcakes

To decorate

100 g / 3 ½ oz / ½ cup butter, softened

200 g / 7 oz / 2 cups icing (confectioners') sugar

½ tsp vanilla extract

200 g / 7 oz ready to roll fondant icing

red, black and blue food colouring

1

- Take 12 vanilla cupcakes ready to decorate.

- Beat the butter until smooth, then gradually whisk in the icing sugar and vanilla extract. Spread the buttercream on top of the cakes, levelling the top with a palette knife.

- Dust the work surface lightly with icing sugar. Colour two thirds of the fondant icing red and roll out it out on the work surface.

- Use a cookie cutter the same diameter as the top of the cakes to cut out 12 circles.

2

- Attach an icing circle to the top of each cake.

- Reserve a small piece of white fondant icing for the eyes then colour the rest black.

3

- Roll out the black icing and use a pizza wheel to cut part of it into 12 thin strips.

4

- Lay one strip down the centre of each cake, securing with a little water.

- Cut 12 circles 5 cm in diameter from the black icing and cut one edge off of each.

5

- Attach the shapes to the cakes to make the ladybirds' heads.

6

- Cut out 48 small circles to make the spots.

- Attach 4 spots to each ladybird with a dab of water.

- Roll out the reserved white icing and cut out 24 small circles for the eyes.

7

- Make the pupils from small circles of fondant coloured blue with food colouring, and attach to the eyes. Stick the eyes to each head.

Caterpillar Cupcakes
Colour the background icing green and add a face to the first cupcake. Arrange the rest of the cupcakes behind it in a curved line.

1

- Take 12 chocolate chip cupcakes ready to decorate.

- Beat the butter until smooth, then gradually whisk in the icing sugar and vanilla extract. Spread the buttercream on top of the cakes, levelling the top with a palette knife.

- Dust the work surface lightly with icing sugar and roll out half of the fondant icing.

2

- Divide the remaining icing into 4 pieces and colour 1 piece light blue, 1 dark blue, 1 red and 1 pink.

- Roll out the coloured icings and use a square cookie cutter to cut each one into squares.

3

- Use a pizza wheel to cut the squares into quarters.

4

- Brush the white fondant sheet lightly with water and arrange the coloured squares on top in a patchwork pattern.

5

- Use a cookie cutter the same diameter as the top of the cakes to cut out 12 circles.

6

- Attach a patchwork circle to the top of each cake.

Harlequin Cupcakes

Cut the coloured icing into diamonds and fit together as before. Pipe lines of black royal icing to mark the edges of the colours.

Patchwork Cupcakes

Makes: **12**
Preparation time: **1 hour 15 minutes**
Cooking time: **15 - 20 minutes**

Ingredients

12 chocolate chip cupcakes

To decorate

100 g / 3 ½ oz / ½ cup butter, softened

200 g / 7 oz / 2 cups icing
(confectioners') sugar

½ tsp vanilla extract

200 g / 7 oz ready to roll fondant icing

red, blue and pink food colouring

One for the Girls

Fondant Cherry Cupcakes

Makes: **12**
Preparation time
1 hour 10 minutes
Cooking time:
15 - 20 minutes

Ingredients

12 chocolate cupcakes

To decorate

100 g / 3 ½ oz / ½ cup butter, softened

200 g / 7 oz / 2 cups icing
(confectioners') sugar

½ tsp vanilla extract

110 g / 4 oz ready to roll fondant icing

red and green food colouring

1

- Take 12 chocolate cupcakes ready to decorate.
- Beat the butter until smooth, then gradually whisk in the icing sugar and vanilla extract.
- Spoon the mixture into a piping bag, fitted with a large star nozzle and pipe a swirl of buttercream on top of each cake.

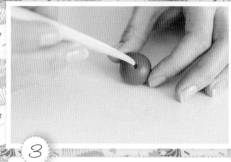

2

- Colour three quarters of the fondant icing red and roll it into 12 balls.

3

- Make an indentation in the top of each one with a veining tool.

4

- Colour the rest of the icing green and roll it into a long thin sausage.

5

- Cut the green icing into 12 cherry stalks.

6

- Sit a cherry on top of each cake and attach the stalks with a dab of water.

Fondant Strawberry Cupcakes

Shape the red icing into 12 strawberry shapes. Roll out the green icing and cut out 12 calyxes with a calyx cutter. Use a little yellow royal icing to pipe on the strawberry seeds.

1

- Take 12 vanilla cupcakes ready to decorate.
- Colour the fondant icing pale pink and roll it out on a work surface.
- Cut out 12 large flowers and 12 medium sized flowers.

2

- Lay the flowers on a foam pad and shape the petals with a ball tool.

4

- Finely chop the rest of the icing off-cuts and add a few drops of water until you can work it into a smooth, pipable icing.
- Colour half of it darker pink and pipe round the edge of the big flowers, adding a dot in the centres. Attach a medium flower to the centre of each large flower.
- Leave the rest of the icing pale and pipe it round the edge of the medium flowers, adding a dot in the centre of each for attaching the icing circles.
- Add an icing dot to the end of each drawn-on stamen.

3

- Briefly knead and then reroll the off-cuts and cut out 12 centres for the flowers with a round cutter. Use the pink food colour pen to draw some stamens in the centre of each one.

5

- Beat the butter until smooth, then gradually whisk in the icing sugar and vanilla extract.
- Spoon the buttercream into a piping bag fitted with a large plain nozzle and pipe a small mound on top of each cake.
- Arrange a flower at an angle on top of each cake.

Purple Flower Cupcakes

Colour the fondant icing purple and dust the petals lightly with gold dusting powder before piping on the edges.

Pink Flower Cupcakes

Makes: **12**

Preparation time:
1 hour 13 minutes

Cooking time: **15 - 20 minutes**

Ingredients

12 vanilla cupcakes

To decorate

200 g / 7 oz ready to roll fondant icing

pink food colouring

pink food colour pen

100 g / 3 ½ oz / ½ cup butter, softened

200 g / 7 oz / 2 cups icing
(confectioners') sugar

½ tsp vanilla extract

Birdcage Cupcakes

Makes: **12**

Preparation time:
1 hour 15 minutes
Cooking time: **15 - 20 minutes**

Ingredients

12 vanilla cupcakes

To decorate

100 g / 3 ½ oz / ½ cup butter, softened

200 g / 7 oz / 2 cups icing (confectioners') sugar

½ tsp vanilla extract

200 g / 7 oz ready to roll fondant icing

pink and brown food colouring

12 small sugar flowers

1

- Take 12 vanilla cupcakes and arrange them on a work surface ready to decorate.
- Beat the butter until smooth, then gradually whisk in the icing sugar and vanilla extract. Reserve a quarter of the buttercream and set aside.
- Spread the rest of the buttercream on top of the cakes.
- Reserve a quarter of the fondant icing and colour the rest pale pink.
- Dust the work surface lightly with icing sugar and roll out the pink fondant icing.

2

- Use a cookie cutter the same diameter as the top of the cakes to cut out 12 circles.
- Attach an icing circle to the top of each cake.

3

- Colour the remaining buttercream brown and spoon it into a piping bag fitted with a small plain nozzle.
- Pipe the outline of a birdcage on top of each cake.

4

- Pipe 4 vertical bars onto each birdcage, followed by a horizontal bar along the top.
- Attach a small sugar flower to the top of each cage while the icing is still wet.

5

- Make doves using a dove shaped mould.

6

- Attach a dove to each cage with a dab of water.

Dog Basket Cupcakes

Use the brown buttercream to pipe a dog basket on top of each cake and use a mould to model a small dog's face to look out of the top of each one.

1

- Take 12 chocolate cupcakes and arrange them on a work surface ready to decorate.
- Top each cake with a thick layer of brown sugar 'sand' and make ripples in it with the spoon handle.

2

- Reserve 1 quarter of the fondant icing and colour the rest red.
- Brush the inside of a silicone flip-flop mould with icing sugar.

3

- Press a small amount of the white icing into the strap details inside the mould, making sure the top is flush with the design.

4

- Press a ball of red icing into each of the mould's indents and press down firmly to flatten.

5

- Turn the mould upside down and peel it away to reveal the icing flip-flops.

6

- Position 2 flip flops on top of each cake.

Beach Cupcakes

Omit the icing flip flops. Colour some royal icing blue and cover half of the top of each cake with an icing wave. Insert a paper umbrella into the 'sand' of each cupcake.

Beach Shoes Cupcakes

Makes: **12**
Preparation time:
1 hour 10 minutes
Cooking time: **15 - 20 minutes**

Ingredients

12 chocolate cupcakes

To decorate

110 g / 4 oz / ½ cup light brown sugar
110 g / 4 oz ready to roll fondant icing
red food colouring

Handbag Cupcakes

Makes: **12**
Preparation time: **1 hour 10 minutes**
Cooking time: **15 - 20 minutes**

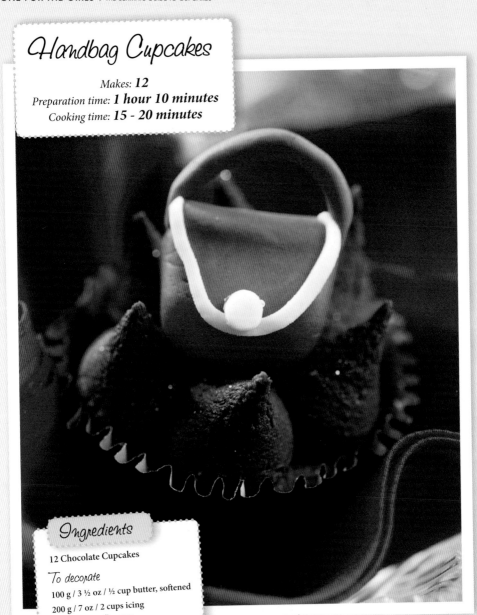

Ingredients

12 Chocolate Cupcakes

To decorate

100 g / 3 ½ oz / ½ cup butter, softened

200 g / 7 oz / 2 cups icing
(confectioners') sugar

1 tbsp unsweetened cocoa powder

200 g / 7 oz ready to roll fondant icing

red food colouring

edible glitter for dusting

1

- Take 12 chocolate cupcakes ready to decorate.
- Beat the butter until smooth, then gradually whisk in the icing sugar and cocoa powder.
- Spoon the mixture into a piping bag, fitted with a large plain nozzle and pipe the buttercream onto the cakes. Dust with edible glitter.
- Reserve a small piece of fondant icing to make the trim and colour the rest red.

2

- Shape the red icing into 12 cubes with your hands.

3

- Using a small rolling pin, flatten one half of each cube.

4

- Use a pizza wheel to cut the flattened side into a curve.
- Fold the flattened curve back over the rest of the cube to form the flap of the bag.

5

- Roll out the reserved white icing and cut it into strips.
- Attach a strip of white icing along the edge of the bag flap with a dab of water.

6

- Use a small plunger cutter to cut out 12 tiny white clasps and attach them to the bags as before.
- Briefly knead the red icing off-cuts together and shape them into 12 handbag straps, then attach to the bags.

7

- Sit the finished handbags in the centre of the cakes.

Satchel Cupcakes

Use the method above to sculpt 12 school satchels out of brown icing.

1

- Take 12 vanilla cupcakes ready to decorate.
- Beat the butter until smooth, then gradually whisk in the icing sugar and vanilla extract.
- Spread the icing onto the cakes, smoothing the tops with a palette knife.

2

- Colour the fondant icing purple and roll it out on a work surface.
- Use a cookie cutter the same diameter as the top of the cakes to cut out 12 circles.

3

- Transfer an icing circle to the top of each cake, smoothing them over with your hands.
- Finely chop the icing off-cuts and transfer them to a bowl. Add warm water a few drops at a time until you can work the mixture into a thick but pipable icing.

4

- Pour the icing into a piping bag fitted with a small plain nozzle.

5

- Pipe filigree swirls over the surface of the cakes.

Monogram Cupcakes

Pipe your guests' initials in elegant script on top of the cakes instead of the filigree swirls.

Filigree Swirl Cupcakes

Makes: **12**
Preparation time:
1 hour 10 minutes
Cooking time: **15 - 20 minutes**

Ingredients

12 vanilla cupcakes

To decorate

100 g / 3 ½ oz / ½ cup butter, softened

200 g / 7 oz / 2 cups icing (confectioners') sugar

½ tsp vanilla extract

200 g / 7 oz ready to roll fondant icing

purple food colouring

Vintage Rose Cupcakes

Makes: **12**
Preparation time: **1 hour**
Cooking time: **15 - 20 minutes**

Ingredients

12 chocolate cupcakes

To decorate

200 g / 7 oz ready to roll fondant icing
blue pearlescent dusting powder

1

- Take 12 chocolate cupcakes ready to decorate.
- Dust the work surface lightly with icing sugar and roll out the fondant icing.

2

- Dust a rose-shaped embossing tool with icing sugar to stop it from sticking.
- Press the embossing tool into the surface of the icing, being careful not to cut all the way through.

3

- Repeat until the surface of the icing is filled with roses.

4

- Use a cookie cutter the same diameter as the top of the cakes to cut out 12 circles.

5

- Using a dry paint brush, work blue pearlescent dusting powder into the embossed lines.

6

- Attach an icing circle to the top of each cake, using a dab of water to secure.

Vintage Lace Cupcakes

Use a lace embossing tool in place of the rose embossing tool.

1

- Take 12 chocolate chip cupcakes ready to decorate.
- Dust the work surface lightly with icing sugar and roll out two thirds of the fondant icing, then use a scalloped edge cookie cutter the same diameter as the top of the cakes to cut out 12 circles.

2

- Attach an icing circle to the top of each cake with a dab of water and reserve the off-cuts.
- Colour the rest of the icing ivory and roll it out. Use a smaller scalloped edge cookie cutter to cut out 12 circles and attach each one to the top of a cake with a dab of water.

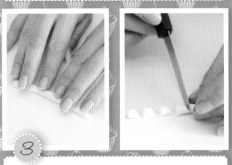

3

- Roll the white icing off-cuts into a 5 mm diameter sausage and cut it into 5mm lengths. Roll each piece of icing into a smooth ball with your hands and transfer to a small bowl.

4

- Sprinkle in some pearlescent dusting powder.
- Swirl the bowl to coat the icing balls in the powder.

5

- Brush the rim of the ivory icing circles with a little water.
- Stick the icing pearls to the top of the cakes in a ring where the icing is wet.

6

- Add a single pearl to the centre of each cake, using water to attach as before.

Black Pearl Cupcakes

Make the pearls out of black icing before rolling in the pearlescent dusting powder.

Pearls Cupcakes

Makes: *12*
Preparation time:
1 hour 30 minutes
Cooking time:
15 - 20 minutes

Ingredients

12 chocolate chip cupcakes

To decorate

400 g / 14 oz ready to roll fondant icing

ivory food colouring

icing (confectioners') sugar for dusting

pearlescent dusting powder

White Chocolate Raspberry Cupcakes

Makes: **12**

Preparation time: **1 hour**

Cooking time: **15 - 20 minutes**

Ingredients

12 vanilla cupcakes

To decorate

100 g / 3 ½ oz / ½ cup butter, softened

200 g / 7 oz / 2 cups icing (confectioners') sugar

4 tbsp raspberry jam (jelly)

96 white chocolate buttons

36 raspberries

1

- Take 12 vanilla cupcakes ready to decorate.
- Beat the butter until smooth, then gradually whisk in the icing sugar and vanilla extract.

2

- Swirl through half of the raspberry jam to create a marbled effect.
- Spread the buttercream onto the cakes with the back of the spoon.

3

- Make an indent in the top of the icing with a teaspoon.

4

- Press 8 white chocolate buttons into the icing round the edge of each cake.

5

- Fill the indentation in the icing with the rest of the raspberry jam and top each one with 3 raspberries.

White Chocolate Blueberry Cupcakes

Use blueberry jam in place of the raspberry jam and use fresh blueberries instead of the raspberries.

Just for fun

1

- Take 12 chocolate cupcakes ready to decorate.
- Beat the butter until smooth, then gradually whisk in the icing sugar and cocoa powder.
- Spoon the mixture into a piping bag, fitted with a large plain nozzle and pipe a swirl of buttercream on top of each cake.

2

- Colour half of the fondant icing red and roll it between your hands into a sausage.
- Roll the sausage backwards and forwards on the work surface until it is 5 mm in diameter.
- Repeat the process with the white icing, reserving a small piece for the leaves.

3

- Brush one side of the white icing with a little water and attach it to the red icing.
- Cut the icing into 10 cm lengths with a pizza wheel.
- Twist the icing strands together and curl round one end to form a candy cane shape. Repeat to make 12 candy canes.

4

- Add a candy cane to the top of each cupcake.

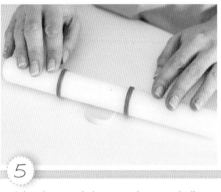

5

- Colour the reserved white icing pale green and roll it out.

6

- Use a holly leaf plunger cutter to cut out 12 leaves and attach 2 leaves to the top of each cake.

Peppermint Candy Cane Cupcakes
Add a few drops of peppermint essence to the cake mixture and knead a few drops into the fondant icing when you add the food colouring.

Chocolate Candy Cane Cupcakes

Makes: **12**
Preparation time: **1 hour 10 minutes**
Cooking time: **15 - 20 minutes**

Ingredients

12 chocolate cupcakes

To decorate

100 g / 3 ½ oz / ½ cup butter, softened

200 g / 7 oz / 2 cups icing (confectioners') sugar

1 tbsp unsweetened cocoa powder

200 g / 7 oz ready to roll fondant icing

red and green food colouring

Shooting Star Cupcakes

Makes: **12**
Preparation time:
1 hour 30 minutes
Cooking time:
15 - 20 minutes

Ingredients

12 vanilla cupcakes

To decorate

100 g / 3 ½ oz / ½ cup butter, softened

200 g / 7 oz / 2 cups icing (confectioners') sugar

½ tsp vanilla extract

200 g / 7 oz ready to roll fondant icing

pink food colouring

48 floral wires

1

- Take 12 vanilla cupcakes ready to decorate.
- Beat the butter until smooth, then gradually whisk in the icing sugar and vanilla extract.
- Spread the buttercream on top of the cakes and smooth the surface with a palette knife.
- Reserve a third of the fondant icing for the stars and colour the rest pink.

2

- Roll out the pink icing on a work surface and cut out 12 circles the same diameter as the top of the cupcakes with a fluted cookie cutter.
- Roll out the white icing.

3

- Cut out 60 medium sized stars and stick one star in the centre of each cake, securing with a dab of water.

4

- Use a small star plunger cutter to cut out 12 tiny stars for each cake and attach them round the outside of the cupcakes as before.

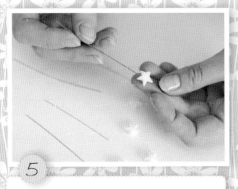

5

- Thread each remaining medium sized star onto a piece of floral wire.

6

- Insert 4 wires into each cake through the star in the centre and fan them out.

Seagull Cupcakes
Use a seagull shaped cutter and thread them onto wires as before. Colour the background icing blue instead of pink and omit the stars.

1

- Take 12 chocolate cupcakes ready to decorate.
- Colour the fondant icing pale green, kneading until all the streaks of colour have disappeared.

2

- Dust the work surface lightly with icing sugar and roll out the icing.

- Cut the icing into long strips with a multi-cutter.

4

- Wrap each strip of icing in a spiral around a wooden dowel and leave to set and harden overnight.
- Beat the butter until smooth, then gradually whisk in the icing sugar and vanilla extract.

5

- Colour the buttercream pale green and spread half of it over the surface of the cakes.
- Spoon the rest of the buttercream into a piping bag, fitted with a plain nozzle and pipe a ring of teardrops round the edge of each cake.

- Sprinkle the centres with green sugar sprinkles.
- When the icing ribbons have hardened, carefully slide them off the dowels and arrange on top of the cakes.

Yellow Ribbon Cupcakes

Colour the fondant icing and butter icing yellow.

Green Ribbon Cupcakes

Makes: **12**

Preparation time:
1 hour 15 minutes
Cooking time: **15 - 20 minutes**
Setting time: **overnight**

Ingredients

12 chocolate cupcakes

To decorate

100 g / 3 ½ oz ready to roll fondant icing

green food colouring

100 g / 3 ½ oz / ½ cup butter, softened

200 g / 7 oz / 2 cups icing
(confectioners') sugar

½ tsp vanilla extract

green sugar sprinkles

Lemon Meringue Cupcakes

Makes: **12**
Preparation time:
1 hour 10 minutes
Cooking time: **15 - 20 minutes**

Ingredients

12 lemon cupcakes

To decorate

100 g / 3 ½ oz / ½ cup lemon curd

200 g / 7 oz / 2 cups marshmallow fluff

1 lemon, cut into 12 wedges

1

- Take 12 lemon cupcakes ready to decorate.
- Use an apple corer to remove the centre of each cupcake.

2

- Fill the cavity in each cupcake with a heaped teaspoon of lemon curd.

3

- Spoon the marshmallow fluff into a piping bag and cover the surface of the cakes with small teardrops.

4

- Use a fork to rough up the top, making sure there are no gaps.

5

- Use a blowtorch to toast the marshmallow topping then top each one with a wedge of lemon.

Baked Alaska Cupcakes

Replace the lemon curd with a small scoop of ice cream then top with the marshmallow fluff and toast as before. Serve immediately.

1

- Take 12 red velvet cupcakes ready to decorate.
- Beat the cream cheese and butter together until light and fluffy then beat in the icing sugar a quarter at a time. Add the vanilla extract then whip the mixture for 2 minutes or until smooth and light.
- Spoon the icing into a piping bag, fitted with a large plain nozzle, and pipe some icing on top of each cake.

2

- Colour the fondant icing red and roll it out on a work surface that has been lightly dusted with icing sugar.

3

- Use a heart-shaped cutter to cut out 60 hearts and attach 5 hearts to the top of each cake like the petals of a flower.

4

- Cut out 12 small circles of icing and attach one to the centre of each cake.

5

- Use a small dry cake brush to apply a little edible glitter to the top of each cake.

Blue Velvet Cupcakes

Replace the red food colouring with blue food colouring in the cake mixture and to colour the fondant icing.

Red Velvet Heart Flower Cupcakes

Makes: **12**
Preparation time: **30 minutes**
Cooking time: **15 minutes**

Ingredients

12 red velvet cupcakes

To decorate

110 g / 4 oz / ½ cup cream cheese

55 g / 2 oz / ¼ cup butter, softened

110 g / 4 oz / 1 cup icing (confectioners') sugar

1 tsp vanilla extract

150 g / 5 ½ oz ready to roll fondant icing

red food colouring

edible glitter

Nautical Cupcakes

Makes: **12**
Preparation time: **1 hour 30 minutes**
Cooking time: **15 - 20 minutes**

Ingredients

12 lemon cupcakes

To decorate

400 g / 14 oz ready to roll fondant icing

blue and red food colouring

icing (confectioners') sugar for dusting

1

- Take 12 lemon cupcakes ready to decorate.
- Colour half of the fondant icing blue. Dust the work surface lightly with icing sugar and roll out the blue icing. Use a cookie cutter the same diameter as the top of the cakes to cut out 12 circles then attach them to the top of the cakes with a dab of water.

2

- Colour half of the remaining icing red and roll it out then cut out 12 circles 5 cm in diameter.

3

- Cut each circle in half with a pizza wheel to make the body of the boats.

4

- Take a slice off of the remaining halves to form the masts and attach the boats and masts to the cakes with a dab of water.

5

- Roll out the remaining white fondant and cut it into 24 triangles for the sails.

6

- Attach 2 sails to each boat, securing with a dab of water.

7

- Reroll the white icing off-cuts and cut out 12 disks with a 1.5 cm round plunger cutter. Cut out the centres with a 5 mm plunger cutter then attach the rings to the top of the cake with a dab of water.

Jolly Rodger Cupcakes

Use black fondant icing for the background and cut a white skull and cross bones for each cake out of white icing.

1

- Take 12 vanilla cupcakes and arrange them on a work surface ready to decorate.

2

- Beat the butter until smooth, then gradually whisk in the icing sugar and vanilla extract. Spread the buttercream on top of the cakes, levelling the top with a palette knife.

3

- Dust the work surface lightly with icing sugar and roll out the fondant icing.
- Use a cookie cutter the same diameter as the top of the cakes to cut out 12 circles.

4

- Attach an icing circle to the top of each cake.

5

- Let down some black food colouring with a few drops of water in a mixing pot.

6

- Use a fine paint brush to paint black stripes onto the white fondant icing.

Tiger Print Cupcakes

Colour the fondant icing orange before rolling it out and topping the cakes. Paint on the black lines as before.

Animal Print Cupcakes

Makes: **12**
Preparation time: **1 hour**
Cooking time: **15 - 20 minutes**

Ingredients

12 vanilla cupcakes

To decorate

100 g / 3 ½ oz / ½ cup butter, softened

200 g / 7 oz / 2 cups icing (confectioners') sugar

½ tsp vanilla extract

200 g / 7 oz ready to roll fondant icing

black food colouring

Nutty Cupcakes

Makes: **12**
Preparation time: **1 hour 10 minutes**
Cooking time: **15 - 20 minutes**

Ingredients

12 vanilla cupcakes

To decorate

100 g / 3 ½ oz / ½ cup butter, softened

200 g / 7 oz / 2 cups icing
(confectioners') sugar

½ tsp vanilla extract

200 g / 7 oz / 1 ½ cups blanched
almonds

1

- Take 12 vanilla cupcakes ready to decorate.
- Beat the butter until smooth, then whisk in the icing sugar and vanilla extract.

2

- Spoon the mixture into a piping bag, fitted with a large plain nozzle and pipe a mound onto each cake.

3

- Reserve 96 almonds for decoration and finely chop the rest.

4

- Dip the cakes in the chopped almonds so that they stick to the buttercream.

5

- Stick 8 whole blanched almonds around the edge of the buttercream like the petals of a flower.

Chocolate Nutty Cupcakes

Add 2 tbsp of cocoa powder to the cake mixture and 1 tbsp of cocoa to the buttercream when you add the icing sugar.

1

- Take 12 chocolate chip cupcakes ready to decorate.
- Beat the butter until smooth, then gradually whisk in the icing sugar and vanilla extract. Spread the buttercream on top of the cakes, levelling the top with a palette knife.

2

- Divide the fondant icing into 6 pieces and colour each piece a different colour.
- Pack the first colour into a sugar paste gun and extrude a plain rope of fondant.

3

- Repeat with the other colours to make the ropes, then stick them together into a sheet with a little water.

4

- Trim the ends with a pizza wheel.

5

- Use a round cookie cutter the same diameter as the top of the cakes to cut the rainbow sheet into 12 rounds.

6

- Transfer each round carefully to the top of a cake with a plastic scraper.

Braided Cupcakes
Braid the fondant ropes together before arranging on top of the cupcakes.

Rainbow Cupcakes

Makes: **12**
Preparation time: **1 hour 15 minutes**
Cooking time: **15 - 20 minutes**

Ingredients

12 chocolate chip cupcakes

To decorate

100 g / 3 ½ oz / ½ cup butter, softened

200 g / 7 oz / 2 cups icing (confectioners') sugar

½ tsp vanilla extract

300 g / 10 ½ oz ready to roll fondant icing

red, orange, yellow, green, blue and purple food colouring

Polka Dot Cupcakes

Makes: **12**
Preparation time:
1 hour 15 minutes
Cooking time:
15 - 20 minutes

Ingredients

12 vanilla cupcakes

To decorate

100 g / 3 ½ oz / ½ cup butter, softened

200 g / 7 oz / 2 cups icing (confectioners') sugar

½ tsp vanilla extract

100 g / 3 ½ oz ready to roll fondant icing

pink and purple food colouring

1

- Take 12 vanilla cupcakes ready to decorate.
- Beat the butter until smooth, then gradually whisk in the icing sugar and vanilla extract.

2

- Spoon the buttercream into a piping bag, fitted with a large star nozzle and pipe a big swirl on top of each cake.

3

- Colour half of the fondant icing pink and the other half purple.

4

- Roll out the icing and use a 1.5 cm plunger cutter to cut circles out of the pink and purple icing.

5

- Transfer the polka dots to the cakes and press them lightly into the buttercream.

Fondant Hearts Cupcakes
Use a heart-shaped plunger cutter to cut out small hearts instead of polka dots.

1

- Take 12 lemon cupcakes, and arrange them ready to decorate.

- Dust the work surface lightly with icing sugar and roll out the blue icing. Use a cookie cutter the same diameter as the cake tops to cut out 12 circles, attach them to the top of the cakes with a dab of water.

2

- Use the same cookie cutter to gauge the correct size for the camper van and make a template out of card.

3

- Take the orange icing, roll it out then use the template to help you cut out 12 van shapes with a scalpel.

4

- Roll out the white icing and cut out 12 more van shapes.

- Stack the white shapes on top of the orange shapes and cut a 'v' through each.

5

- Assemble the vans on top of the cakes, using the white tops and the orange bottoms, attaching with a dab of water.

- Use a round plunger cutter to cut circles out of the orange icing off-cuts and attach them to the campervans.

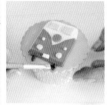

6

- Roll out the yellow fondant and use a plunger cutter to make the headlights and indicators.

- Knead the remaining white off-cuts with the blue off-cuts to make a pale blue icing, then cut out and attach the windows and number plate.

7

- Roll out the red fondant then cut out and attach a bumper to each van.

- The tires can be painted directly onto the cakes using a little black food colouring and a small paint brush.

Beetle Cupcakes

Make a card template of the side profile of a VW Beetle and cut out and attach the fondant icing as before.

Campervan Cupcakes

Makes: **12**
Preparation time: **1 hour 30 minutes**
Cooking time: **15 - 20 minutes**

Ingredients

12 lemon cupcakes

To decorate

400 g / 14 oz ready to roll fondant icing

blue, orange, yellow, red and
black food colouring

icing (confectioners') sugar for dusting

Occasions

Black and White Cupcakes

Makes: **12**
Preparation time: **1 hour**
Cooking time: **15 - 20 minutes**

Ingredients

12 vanilla cupcakes

To decorate

100 g / 3 ½ oz / ½ cup butter, softened

200 g / 7 oz / 2 cups icing
(confectioners') sugar

½ tsp vanilla extract

200 g / 7 oz ready to roll fondant icing

black food colouring

1

- Take 12 vanilla cupcakes and arrange them on a work surface ready to decorate.
- Beat the butter until smooth, then gradually whisk in the icing sugar and vanilla extract. Spread the buttercream on the cake tops, levelling with a palette knife.

2

- Dust the work surface lightly with icing sugar and roll out two thirds of the fondant icing.

3

- Use a cookie cutter the same diameter as the top of the cakes to cut out 12 circles.

4

- Attach an icing circle to the top of each cake.
- Colour the remaining icing black, divide it in half and roll it out into 2 long strips on the work surface.

5

- Slice one piece into 5 mm slices with a pizza wheel.
- Cut out 5 mm circles from the other piece with a small plunger cutter.

6

- Lay 4 strips of black icing across the top of each cake, securing with a dab of water.
- Cut off the edges of the black icing strips with a sharp knife.

7

- Add a row of black dots between 2 of the strips of black icing, securing with a little water.

Checkerboard Cupcakes

Cut the white icing and black icing into squares and alternate them on top of the cakes in a checkerboard pattern.

1

- Take 12 chocolate cupcakes ready to decorate.
- Beat the butter until smooth, then gradually whisk in the icing sugar and vanilla extract.
- Spoon the mixture into a piping bag, fitted with a large star nozzle and pipe a swirl of buttercream on top of each cake.

2

- Roll out the fondant icing until 4 mm thick.

3

- Cut out 12 circles with a 2 cm diameter plunger cutter.

4

- Cut out the centres with a 1.5 cm plunger cutter and leave to harden overnight.

5

- Attach a pink sugar ball 'jewel' to the top of each icing ring with a dab of water, then transfer the rings to the cakes.

6

Wedding Ring Cupcakes

After the rings have hardened, spray them with edible gold paint and leave to dry before topping the cakes.

Engagement Ring Cupcakes

Makes: **12**
Preparation time:
1 hour 10 minutes
Cooking time: **15 - 20 minutes**
Setting time: **overnight**

Ingredients

12 chocolate cupcakes

To decorate

100 g / 3 ½ oz / ½ cup butter, softened
200 g / 7 oz / 2 cups icing (confectioners') sugar
½ tsp vanilla extract
100 g / 3 ½ oz ready to roll fondant icing
12 pink sugar balls

Dove Cupcakes

Makes: **12**
Preparation time: **1 hour**
Cooking time: **15 - 20 minutes**

Ingredients

12 vanilla cupcakes

To decorate

100 g / 3 ½ oz / ½ cup butter, softened

200 g / 7 oz / 2 cups icing (confectioners') sugar

½ tsp vanilla extract

200 g / 7 oz ready to roll fondant icing

ivory food colouring

1

- Take 12 vanilla cupcakes ready to decorate.

- Beat the butter until smooth, then gradually whisk in the icing sugar and vanilla extract. Spread the buttercream on top of the cakes, levelling the top with a palette knife.

2

- Dust the work surface lightly with icing sugar and roll out three quarters of the fondant icing.

3

- Use a cookie cutter the same diameter as the top of the cakes to cut out 12 circles.

- Attach an icing circle to the top of each cake.

4

- Colour the rest of the icing a pale ivory colour.

- Dust the inside of a dove-shaped mould with a little icing sugar.

5

- Press a small ball of icing into the mould, making sure it goes into every corner.

- Carefully turn out the dove onto the work surface and repeat the process to make 12 doves in total.

6

- Attach a dove to the top of each cake with a dab of water.

Horseshoe Cupcakes

Colour the icing silver instead of ivory and use a horseshoe shaped mould to make the cake toppers.

1

- Take 12 lemon cupcakes ready to decorate.
- Reserve a small piece of fondant icing for the stalks and colour the rest orange.

2

- Divide the orange fondant icing into 12 pieces and roll into balls with your hands.

3

- Use a paring knife to score each ball into segments.

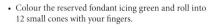

4

- Use a ball tool to make a dip in the top and slightly flatten each ball.
- Colour the reserved fondant icing green and roll into 12 small cones with your fingers.

5

- Attach the stalks to the pumpkins with a dab of water.
- Beat the butter until smooth, then gradually whisk in the icing sugar and lemon juice.

6

- Spoon half the mixture into a piping bag, fitted with a large plain nozzle and pipe a mound of buttercream on top of each cake. Sprinkle with ground cinnamon.
- Colour the rest of the buttercream orange and spoon it into a piping bag fitted with a plain nozzle.

7

- Pipe a ring of teardrops round the outside of the plain buttercream, then position a pumpkin on top of each cake.

Halloween Lantern Cupcakes

Cut eyes and mouths out of black fondant icing and attach them to the pumpkins with a dab of water.

Halloween Cupcakes

Makes: **12**
Preparation time:
1 hour 20 minutes
Cooking time:
15 - 20 minutes

Ingredients

12 lemon cupcakes

To decorate

200 g / 7 oz ready to roll fondant icing

orange and green food colouring

100 g / 3 ½ oz / ½ cup butter, softened

200 g / 7 oz / 2 cups icing (confectioners') sugar

1 tbsp lemon juice

½ tsp ground cinnamon

Christmas Tree Cupcakes

Makes: **12**
Preparation time: **1 hour 15 minutes**
Cooking time: **15 - 20 minutes**

Ingredients

12 vanilla cupcakes

To decorate

100 g / 3 ½ oz / ½ cup butter, softened

200 g / 7 oz / 2 cups icing (confectioners') sugar

½ tsp vanilla extract

orange, red and green food colouring

200 g / 7 oz ready to roll fondant icing

coloured sugar balls to decorate

1

- Take 12 vanilla cupcakes ready to decorate.
- Beat the butter until smooth, then gradually whisk in the icing sugar and vanilla extract.
- Colour the buttercream orange, then swirl through a few drops of red food colouring to create a marbled effect.
- Spoon the buttercream into a piping bag, fitted with a large star nozzle and pipe a big swirl on top of each cake.

2

- Colour the fondant icing green and shape it into 12 balls.

3

- Roll each ball between your hands, adding more pressure to one side to form a cone.

4

- Insert a cocktail stick into the thick end of each cone.

5

- Holding the cones by their cocktail sticks, use a pair of clean nail scissors to snip 'v' shapes into the outside.
- Use a dab of water to attach coloured sugar balls to make the baubles.

6

- Carefully remove the cocktail sticks and press a Christmas tree into the buttercream on top of each cake.

Pinecone Cupcakes
Use the scissor sniping method to make pinecones out of brown fondant icing.

1

- Take 12 lemon cupcakes ready to decorate.
- Roll out the fondant icing thickly on a work surface that has been dusted with icing sugar.

2

- Dust the inside of a snowflake plunger cutter with icing sugar to stop it from sticking.
- Cut out 12 snowflakes and leave them to dry and harden overnight.

3

- The next day, paint the snowflakes silver and leave to dry for a few minutes.

4

- Beat the butter until smooth, then gradually whisk in the icing sugar and vanilla extract.

5

- Spoon the mixture into a piping bag, fitted with a large star nozzle and pipe a swirl of buttercream on top of each cake.

6

- Arrange a snowflake on top of each cake and decorate with silver balls.

Gold Star Cupcakes
Cut large stars out of the fondant icing and leave to set as before. Paint with gold food colouring and arrange on top of the cupcakes.

Silver Snowflake Cupcakes

Makes: **12**
Preparation time: **1 hour 10 minutes**
Cooking time: **15 - 20 minutes**
Setting time: **overnight**

Ingredients

12 lemon cupcakes

To decorate

100 g / 3 ½ oz / ½ cup butter, softened

200 g / 7 oz / 2 cups icing (confectioners') sugar

½ tsp vanilla extract

150 g / 5 ⅓ oz ready to roll fondant icing

silver food colouring

edible silver balls

Easter Basket Cupcakes

Makes: **12**
Preparation time: **1 hour 10 minutes**
Cooking time: **15 - 20 minutes**

Ingredients

12 vanilla cupcakes

To decorate

100 g / 3 ½ oz / ½ cup butter, softened

200 g / 7 oz / 2 cups icing (confectioners') sugar

1 tbsp unsweetened cocoa powder

72 chocolate mini eggs

1

- Take 12 vanilla cupcakes ready to decorate.
- Beat the butter until smooth, then add the icing sugar and cocoa powder to the bowl.

2

- Beat the mixture with a wooden spoon to make a smooth chocolate buttercream.

3

- Spoon the mixture into a piping bag, fitted with a large basket weave nozzle and pipe an undulating ring of icing on top of each cake.

4

- Arrange 6 chocolate mini eggs on top of each cake.

Easter Nest Cupcakes
Use a small plain nozzle to pipe squiggles of icing on top of each cake to make a nest.

1

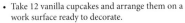

- Take 12 vanilla cupcakes and arrange them on a work surface ready to decorate.
- Colour half of the fondant icing bright blue. Dust the work surface lightly with icing sugar and roll out the blue icing. Use a cookie cutter the same diameter as the top of the cakes to cut out 12 circles then attach them to the top of the cakes with a dab of water.
- Reserve a small piece of the white fondant icing for the flowers and colour the rest pale blue.

2

- Roll the pale blue icing into 12 balls.
- Cut a third of the icing off of each ball and reserve.

3

- Shape the remaining two thirds of each ball into pear shapes.
- Dip a ball tool into icing sugar to stop it from sticking, then make a hollow in the thinner end of each pear shape.

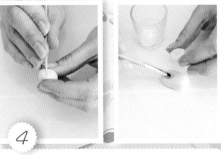

4

- Roll the remaining third of each ball into a thick disk and use a cocktail stick to make indentations round the outside.
- Attach each disk to the top of a boot with a little water and hollow the insides with a smaller ball tool.

5

- Use the end of a small star nozzle to make an imprint on the front of each boot.
- Roll out the reserved white icing and cut out 12 small flowers with a plunger cutter and attach to the top of the cakes with a dab of water.

6

- Use some of the bright blue icing off-cuts to make the flower centres.
- Attach a boot to the top of each cake with a drop of water.

Swaddled Baby Cupcakes

Make 12 long pink cone shapes out of pale pink icing and swaddle each one in a sheet of blue icing. Paint the facial features onto each baby with a little brown food colouring.

Baby Boots Cupcakes

Makes: **12**
Preparation time:
1 hour 15 minutes
Cooking time:
15 - 20 minutes

Ingredients

12 vanilla cupcakes

To decorate

400 g / 14 oz ready to roll fondant icing

blue food colouring

icing (confectioners') sugar for dusting

Blue Baby Feet Cupcakes

Makes: **12**
Preparation time: **1 hour 10 minutes**
Cooking time: **15 - 20 minutes**

Ingredients

12 lemon cupcakes

To decorate

400 g / 14 oz ready to roll fondant icing

blue and pink food colouring

icing (confectioners') sugar for dusting

1

- Take 12 lemon cupcakes ready to decorate.
- Colour two thirds of the fondant icing blue. Dust the work surface lightly with icing sugar and roll out the blue icing. Use a cookie cutter the same diameter as the cake tops to cut out 12 circles, attach them to the top of the cakes with a dab of water.
- Finely chop the remaining white fondant icing and put it in a small bowl. Gradually work in warm water a few drops at a time until you have a thick, pipable icing.

2

- Add a tiny amount of pink food colouring to turn the icing flesh coloured.

3

- Spoon half of the icing into a piping bag fitted with a flat nozzle and pipe 2 feet onto each cake.

4

- Spoon the rest of the icing into a piping bag with a small plain nozzle and pipe on the toes.

5

- Use a damp paint brush to tidy up the edges of the icing to give a smooth outline.

6

- Use a damp paint brush to flatten down the tops of the dots to remove any points.

Pink Baby Feet Cupcakes

Colour the background icing pink instead of blue.

1

- Take 12 chocolate cupcakes ready to decorate.
- Dust the work surface and roll out 2 thirds of the fondant icing.
- Cut it into 12 squares with a pizza wheel.

2

- Roll each square loosely around the handle of a paint brush to make the scrolls, then leave to set overnight.
- Reserve a small piece of the remaining fondant icing and colour the rest purple.

3

- Cut it into 12 thin ribbons with a pizza wheel.
- Cut a 'v' out of each end of the ribbons with a scalpel.
- Wrap each ribbon around one of the icing scrolls, securing with a dab of water.

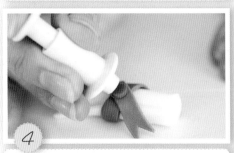

4

- Colour the reserved icing pink and roll it out, then use a plunger cutter to cut out 12 small discs and attach to the ribbons.
- Beat the butter until smooth, then whisk in the icing sugar and vanilla extract.

5

- Colour the buttercream purple then spread half of it over the surface of the cakes and sprinkle with sugar sprinkles.
- Spoon the rest of the buttercream into a piping bag, fitted with a star nozzle and pipe a ring of rosettes round the edge of each cake.

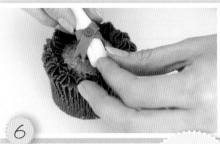

6

- Position the fondant scrolls in the centre of the cakes.

Mortarboard Cupcakes

Colour the fondant icing black and mould it into the shape of 12 mortarboard graduation hats.

Graduation Cupcakes

Makes: **12**
Preparation time: **1 hour 30 minutes**
Cooking time: **15 - 20 minutes**
Setting time: **overnight**

Ingredients

12 chocolate cupcakes

To decorate

100 g / 3 ½ oz ready to roll fondant icing

purple and pink food colouring

100 g / 3 ½ oz / ½ cup butter, softened

200 g / 7 oz / 2 cups icing (confectioners') sugar

½ tsp vanilla extract

purple sugar sprinkles

Birthdays

Sweeties Cupcakes

Makes: **12**
Preparation time: **1 hour**
Cooking time:
15 - 20 minutes

Ingredients

12 lemon cupcakes

To decorate

100 g / 3 ½ oz / ½ cup butter, softened

200 g / 7 oz / 2 cups icing (confectioners') sugar

½ tsp vanilla extract

12 packets of Parma Violets

36 strawberry jelly sweets

1

- Take 12 lemon cupcakes ready to decorate.
- Beat the butter until smooth, then gradually whisk in the icing sugar and vanilla extract.

2

- Spoon the mixture into a piping bag, fitted with a large star nozzle and use 2 thirds of the buttercream to pipe a rosette on top of each cake.

3

- Open the packets of Parma Violets and press them round the outside of the buttercream rosette.

4

- Pipe the remaining buttercream into a rosette on top of each cake.

5

- Top each cake with 3 strawberry jelly sweets.

Jelly Baby Cupcakes

Top the buttercream with Jelly Babies instead of the Parma Violets and strawberry sweets.

1

- Take 12 lemon cupcakes and arrange them on a work surface ready to decorate.
- Colour half of the fondant icing blue. Dust the work surface lightly with icing sugar and roll out the blue icing. Use a cookie cutter the same diameter as the top of the cakes to cut out 12 circles then attach them to the top of the cakes with a dab of water.

2

- Roll out the white fondant icing until 2 mm thick.

3

- Use a large flower-shaped cutter to cut out 12 flowers.

4

- Attach a flower to the top of each cake, securing with a dab of water.

5

- Briefly knead the blue icing off-cuts and roll them out until 4 mm thick.

6

- Use a number-shaped cutter to cut out 12 numbers.

7

- Brush the back of each number with a little water, then attach one to the centre of each flower.

Alphabet Cupcakes

Use letter-shaped cutters to cut out a different letter for the top of each cake.

Age Cupcakes

Makes: **12**
Preparation time: **1 hour**
Cooking time: **15 - 20 minutes**

Ingredients

12 lemon cupcakes

To decorate

400 g / 14 oz ready to roll fondant icing
blue food colouring
icing (confectioners') sugar for dusting

Candles Cupcakes

Makes: **12**
Preparation time: **1 hour**
Cooking time: **15 - 20 minutes**

Ingredients

12 vanilla cupcakes

To decorate

100 g / 3 ½ oz / ½ cup butter, softened

200 g / 7 oz / 2 cups icing (confectioners') sugar

½ tsp vanilla extract

edible pink glitter

96 birthday candles

96 candle holders

1

- Take 12 vanilla cupcakes and arrange on a work surface ready to decorate.
- Beat the butter until smooth, then gradually whisk in the icing sugar and vanilla extract.
- Spoon the icing into a piping bag fitted with a large star nozzle.

2

- Pipe 8 rosettes of icing on top of each cake.

3

- Use a dry paint brush to sprinkle a little pink edible glitter over the top of each cake.

4

- Insert each candle into a candle holder.

5

- Stick a candle in the top of each icing rosette and light them just before serving.

Sparklers Cupcakes
Use 12 indoor cake sparklers in place of the candles.

1

- Take 12 lemon cupcakes ready to decorate.
- Beat the butter until smooth, then gradually whisk in the icing sugar and vanilla extract.
- Spoon the buttercream into a piping bag, with a large star nozzle and pipe a big swirl on top of each cake.
- Reserve a small amount of icing to make the ribbons and colour the rest pink.
- Roll the pink icing into 12 balls with your hands.

2

- Cut the sides off of the balls to make them into cubes.
- Smooth the edges and sharpen the edges with your hands.

3

- Roll out the reserved white icing and cut it into thin ribbons with a pizza wheel.
- Paint a cross on top of each cube with a little water.

4

- Lay 2 white fondant ribbons across each box and smooth them down the sides. Trim off the ends with a scalpel.

5

- Make 12 tiny bows from the remaining white fondant ribbons.
- Attach the bows to the top of the presents with a dab of water.

6

- Roll some of the pink icing off-cuts into 12 tiny balls and use as the centres of the bows.
- Position a present on top of each cupcake.

Chocolate Present Cupcakes

Add 2 tbsp of cocoa powder to the cake mixture and sprinkle the buttercream with chocolate chips before topping with the presents.

Presents Cupcakes

Makes: **12**
Preparation time:
1 hour 15 minutes
Cooking time:
15 - 20 minutes

Ingredients

12 lemon cupcakes

To decorate

100 g / 3 ½ oz / ½ cup butter, softened
200 g / 7 oz / 2 cups icing (confectioners') sugar
½ tsp vanilla extract
300 g / 9 oz ready to roll fondant icing
pink food colouring

Key Cupcakes

Makes: **12**
Preparation time: **1 hour**
Cooking time: **15 - 20 minutes**

Ingredients

12 vanilla cupcakes

To decorate

200 g / 7 oz ready to roll fondant icing

purple food colouring

100 g / 3 ½ oz ready to pipe royal icing

1

- Take 12 vanilla cupcakes ready to decorate.
- Colour the fondant icing purple with the food colouring. Dust the work surface lightly with icing sugar and roll out the purple icing.

2

- Use a cookie cutter the same diameter as the top of the cakes to cut out 12 circles.
- Attach an icing circle to the top of each cake with a dab of water.

3

- Spoon the royal icing into a piping bag fitted with a small plain nozzle.
- Pipe a key on top of each cake: start with a circle to make the handle, followed by a straight line for the shaft.

4

- Pipe on the teeth of the key.

5

- Finish the cakes by piping a ring of dots around the outer edge.

New House Cupcakes

Use the same method to pipe the outline of a house on top of each cake.

117

1

- Take 12 lemon cupcakes ready to decorate.
- Dust the work surface lightly with icing sugar and roll out half of the fondant icing, then use a cookie cutter the same diameter as the top of the cakes to cut out 12 circles.

2

- Attach an icing circle to the top of each cake with a dab of water.
- Divide the remaining fondant icing into 4 pieces and colour each one a different colour.

3

- Roll out the coloured icings and use a 2 cm diameter round plunger cutter to cut out circles.

4

- Use a 1 cm diameter round plunger cutter to cut circles out of the 2 cm rounds, off-setting the centres as you do so.

5

- Use a dab of water to attach the rings and cut-out centres to the top of the cakes.

Peacock Feather Cupcakes

Use the method above to make icing peacock feathers with a blue centre, gold ring and brown background. Use scissors to feather the edge of the brown icing.

Colours Cupcakes

Makes: **12**
Preparation time: **1 hour 30 minutes**
Cooking time: **15 - 20 minutes**

Ingredients

12 lemon cupcakes

To decorate

400 g / 14 oz ready to roll fondant icing
blue, purple, pink and orange food colouring
icing (confectioners') sugar for dusting

Pink Champagne Cupcakes

Makes: **12**
Preparation time: **1 hour 10 minutes**
Cooking time: **15 - 20 minutes**

Ingredients

12 lemon cupcakes

To decorate

100 g / 3 ½ oz / ½ cup butter, softened

200 g / 7 oz / 2 cups icing (confectioners') sugar

½ tsp vanilla extract

110 g / 4 oz ready to roll fondant icing

pink food colouring

1

- Take 12 lemon cupcakes ready to decorate.
- Reserve a small amount of icing for the labels and colour the rest pink.

2

- Shape the pink icing into 12 bottle shapes.

3

- Roll out the white icing until very thin.

4

- Cut out 12 labels with a scalpel and attach them to the bottles with a dab of water.

5

- Roll the off-cuts into 12 small corks and attach each one to the top of a bottle with a dab of water.

6

- Beat the butter until smooth, then gradually whisk in the icing sugar and vanilla extract.
- Spoon the mixture into a piping bag, fitted with a large star nozzle and pipe 2 large rosettes of buttercream on top of each other on each cake.

7

- Press a champagne bottle into the top of each cake.

Beer Bottle Cupcakes

Colour the icing dark green or brown instead of pink and shape it into 12 beer bottles.

1

- Take 12 vanilla cupcakes and arrange them on a work surface.

- Beat the butter until smooth, then gradually whisk in the icing sugar and vanilla extract. Spread half of the buttercream on top of the cakes, levelling the top with a palette knife.

2

- Colour the fondant icing red and roll it out on the work surface.

- Use a teapot-shaped cookie cutter to cut out 12 teapots.

3

- Carefully transfer the teapots to the top of the cakes, making sure the shape does not distort.

4

- Spoon the rest of the buttercream into a piping bag fitted with a small plain nozzle and pipe the outline onto each teapot.

5

- Pipe dots onto the teapots to decorate.

Coffee Pot Cupcakes
Flavour the cake mixture with 2 tsp of instant espresso powder and use a coffee pot shaped cookie cutter to make the decoration.

Afternoon Tea Cupcakes

Makes: **12**
Preparation time: **1 hour 15 minutes**
Cooking time: **15 - 20 minutes**

Ingredients

12 vanilla cupcakes

To decorate

100 g / 3 ½ oz / ½ cup butter, softened
200 g / 7 oz / 2 cups icing (confectioners') sugar
½ tsp vanilla extract
200 g / 7 oz ready to roll fondant icing
red food colouring

Chocolate Decadence Cupcakes

Makes: **12**
Preparation time:
1 hour 10 minutes
Cooking time:
15 - 20 minutes

Ingredients

12 chocolate cupcakes

To decorate

100 g / 3 ½ oz / ½ cup butter, softened

200 g / 7 oz / 2 cups icing (confectioners') sugar

1 tbsp unsweetened cocoa powder

100 g / 3 ½ oz dark chocolate, melted

48 chocolate malt balls

48 chocolate buttons

1

- Take 12 chocolate cupcakes ready to decorate.
- Beat the butter until smooth, then gradually whisk in the icing sugar and cocoa powder.
- Spoon a quarter of the buttercream into a separate bowl and set aside. Fold the melted chocolate into the rest of the buttercream until smoothly combined.

2

- Spoon the dark chocolate buttercream into a piping bag, fitted with a large plain nozzle and pipe a swirl of buttercream on top of each cake.

3

- Spoon the reserved paler buttercream into a piping bag fitted with a large star nozzle and pipe a rosette on top of each dark chocolate swirl.

Chocolate Orange Decadence Cupcakes

Add the grated zest of an orange to the cake mixture and buttercream. Use strips of candied orange peel to decorate the cakes along with the Maltesers and buttons.

4

- Arrange 4 Maltesers on top of each cake.

5

- Slide a chocolate button between each Malteser.

1

- Take 12 chocolate chip cupcakes ready to decorate.
- Beat the butter until smooth, then gradually whisk in the icing sugar and vanilla extract.
- Spread the buttercream on top of the cakes and smooth the surface with a palette knife.
- Reserve a small piece of fondant icing for the flowers and colour the rest pink.

2

- Roll out 2 thirds of the pink icing on a work surface and cut out 12 circles the same diameter as the top of the cupcakes with a fluted cookie cutter.
- Shape a third of the remaining pink icing into 12 flattened balls and attach to the cakes with a dab of water.

3

- Roll out the rest of the pink icing and cut it into 1 cm thick ribbons.
- Cut 2 short lengths for each cake and cut off the ends on the diagonal.

4

- Attach the tails of the bow to the cakes with a dab of water.

5

- Make the remaining ribbons into 48 loops and attach 4 loops to each cake with cocktail sticks.

6

- Colour the remaining icing pale pink and cut out 12 flower shapes.
- Transfer them to a foam board and use a ball tool to cup the petals.
- Let down any dark pink icing off-cuts with a little water and pipe it in small dots in the centre of the flowers.
- Attach 1 flower to the centre of each bow with a dab of water.

Yellow Bow Cupcakes
Colour the icing yellow instead of pink and make yellow daffodils for the centre of each cake.

Pink Bow Cupcakes

Makes: **12**
Preparation time:
1 hour 30 minutes
Cooking time:
15 - 20 minutes

Ingredients

12 chocolate chip cupcakes

To decorate

100 g / 3 ½ oz / ½ cup butter, softened

200 g / 7 oz / 2 cups icing
(confectioners') sugar

½ tsp vanilla extract

200 g / 7 oz ready to roll fondant icing

pink food colouring

Index